re:action

Jesus: The Sequel

Is he really coming back?

Kate Hayes

**small group Bible resources from
Scripture Union**

## JESUS: THE SEQUEL

Published by Scripture Union, 207–209 Queensway, Bletchley, MK2 2EB, England.

Scripture Union: We are an international Christian charity working with churches in more than 130 countries providing resources to bring the good news about Jesus Christ to children, young people and families – and to encourage them to develop spiritually through the Bible and prayer. As well as our network of volunteers, staff and associates who run holidays, church-based events and school Christian groups, we produce a wide range of publications and support those who use our resources through training programmes.

Email: info@scriptureunion.org.uk
Internet: http://www.scriptureunion.org.uk

First published 2002

ISBN 1 85999 621 3

Scripture taken from the *New Living Translation*, British text, published by Tyndale House Publishers, Inc, Wheaton, Illinois, USA, and distributed by STL Ltd, Carlisle, Cumbria, England; and from *The Message* © Eugene H Peterson, used by permission of NavPress Publishing Group.

British Library Cataloguing-in-Publication Data: a catalogue record for this book is available from the British Library.

Cover design and photography by David Lund Design, Milton Keynes.

Illustrations by Helen Gale.

Printed and bound in Great Britain by Ebenezer Baylis & Son Ltd, The Trinity Press, London Road, Worcester WR5 2JH.

# Contents

# Welcome!

Welcome to **re:action** discussion guides for small groups!

What are the distinctives of **re:action**? The series is strong on links into the contemporary world and concerned that God's Word impacts our everyday lives in practical ways. Understanding the truth leads to a response in the heart and mind of the individual. The sessions encourage personal discovery through actively exploring the Bible but, unlike many group Bible studies on the market, **re:action** assumes little if any prior Bible knowledge. As such it is excellent for those new to looking at Christianity, but that is not to say that the series is lightweight or lacking in depth. More mature Christians will find the series refreshing. The quality of questions should produce lively and thinking debate, and opportunities to share personal experiences. Though some humour is used, especially in the icebreaker **set the scene** sections, the content of the sessions overall is demanding and personally challenging.

Kate Hayes began writing the series out of a sense of frustration with existing materials, and everything she produces has been tried and tested in her own church groups. She says: 'Most study notes are frankly boring. Too many work on a 'the answer must be Jesus' principle, regurgitating bits of text for answers. Others don't seem to relate the learning so as to make a difference to people's everyday lives. I don't write these notes because I want people to find answers to academic questions or clock up the books they've studied and then move on to something else, but because I want to see people grow in understanding and maturity. I want them to find out things that will make a difference every day of their lives, when work is tough, when friends let them down, their lives fall apart and they're faced with living as Christians in our postmodern society.'

Each title in the series contains material for seven sessions. **Preview** is an introductory session that ideally would take place in a social setting, perhaps following a potluck supper or around desserts and coffee. Each session begins with **set the scene**, a light discussion opener, sometimes in the form of a quiz or game, or some fun questions. The **explore** section takes the group into the Bible text, while the **reflect** section moves into the area of personal application. Note that while most of the questions are for group discussion, there are also periods of quiet for tackling personal questions, which don't have to be shared more widely. In the closing **re:action** section there is opportunity to pray through what's been discussed and discovered, and sometimes suggestions for other actions both within and outside the group times.

What about leadership of the group? The **re:action** series is aimed at thinking people willing to be pro-active in searching the Scriptures and discussing their implications. As such, the leadership of the group, by one or two members, can be run with a light touch. The role of the **re:action** group leader is that of a guide through the discussion material rather than a teacher. The leader will sensitively encourage the sharing of answers and personal experiences at an appropriate level. Many questions need just one word answers and can be moved through quite quickly; at other times some brainstorming of ideas would be an appropriate response to the questions; sometimes it will be a more measured and thoughtful discussion. The leader will need to make decisions about when tangents to the discussion are legitimate and when they distract.

Ideally everyone should have their own copy of the booklet and follow through the material together. It's essential for everyone to bring a Bible, as much of the time will be spent around open Bibles. Any translation is fine, and it's often useful to compare different versions. For those new to Bible study, several contemporary translations are to be recommended: the Good News Bible, the Contemporary English Version, or the New Living Translation – and it's the NLT which is used in the booklet whenever Bible text is quoted. It will be useful to have a supply of pens, paper and perhaps card available.

## About the author

Kate Hayes, born into a non-churchgoing family in Sheffield, decided to become a Christian aged 12 after being 'dragged along' to a Pathfinder meeting by a friend. After studying Psychology she did teacher training but then found herself working in bookshops and in software testing for the book trade. In 1994 she moved to Dukinfield in Greater Manchester, where she now coordinates and writes materials for small groups in St John's Church.

# Intro

It's hardly surprising that most of us tend to be almost exclusively pre-occupied with the day to day. Arguably, life is more demanding than ever. The speed of change in technology and communications have impacted our daily routines, so that appointments and tight deadlines come ever faster and closer together.

On the bigger stage, our world faces possible terminal dangers from environmental change, meteorites, biological and chemical terrorism and nuclear war to mention but a few.

As the millennium approached, people ranging from the truly wild and wacky edges of life through to those from some of the established churches suggested that the year 2000 would mark either the return of Jesus or at least an alien invasion. Films such as *Armageddon*, *Deep Impact* and *Independence Day* built interest in possible doomsday scenarios.

So it's understandable, if not excusable, that so much of our thought and energy is consumed by the concerns of the day – what we will eat, how we will get money, who we will spend our time with. And the future, personal or international, gets put in the 'pending' tray. Some people live entirely for the present. Others do spend much of their time planning for or worrying about the future – but it's for a very limited future that revolves around plans for holidays, training for career promotion, or wrestling with pension plans to provide for old age.

How many of us, even those who believe in God, give much thought to life after death – to what we might expect to happen to us, and to how we should be preparing for it today?

Heaven, like the devil in his red tights and horns, has a bit of an image problem. Too many jokes about clouds, pearly gates and angels with wings, white nighties and harps have had an effect. We are dismissive of heaven, or see it as a charming fantasy totally irrelevant to the here and now. As Laurie Lee has said in an essay on 'Paradise', these images have made heaven of no effect: 'Too chaste, too disinfected, too much on its best behaviour, it received little more than a dutiful nod from the faithful.'

The truth is that we are living in that period of history between the two comings to earth of Jesus Christ, a time the Bible calls the Last Days. The first coming happened two thousand years ago. The date of the Second Coming is unknown, though as a fact it is solid certainty. It might happen before your next holiday, your next baby, your next house move, your next... meal? Or maybe not. But either way, doesn't it make sense to give a little thought to it all?

# 1 Preview

## set the scene

You're eight years old and desperate for a special event such as a birthday or holiday to arrive.

Q: Is it coming quickly or slowly?

Q: How do you feel about the wait?

We measure the passing of time very precisely. Every second lasts exactly as long as the one before it and the one after it. However, it often doesn't feel that way. Sometimes time seems to pass very slowly indeed.

Q: When recently have you experienced time going slowly?

Q: When recently have you experienced time going quickly?

Q: What kind of things alter the apparent speed of time?

Q: What about now? In your life generally, are you finding time moving slowly or quickly at the moment? Why is that?

## 1 Looking at time

We live in a world that is built on careful measurement of time. Timetables, working hours, opening hours, appointments, meetings... However, not everything is controlled by time.

Q: What do these Bible verses tell us about time?

Some of them have the same message. Everyone in the group could take a different verse to look up, then discuss your findings as you go through them one by one.

**Read**

Psalm 90:2
Genesis 1:1–5,14
Genesis 6:3
Psalm 39:4
Psalm 90:10,12
1 Peter 4:7
Matthew 24:3,14
Luke 18:26–30
John 3:16

## 2 Looking to the future

*But instead, you dance and play; you slaughter sacrificial animals, feast on meat, and drink wine. 'Let's eat, drink, and be merry,' you say. 'What's the difference, for tomorrow we die.'*
**Isaiah 22:13**

Q: In what ways do you spend today's time planning for the future? (eg insurance, health, finances...)

Some people try to find out what will happen to them in the future

Q: How might they do this?

re:action

## Read

Isaiah 8:19
Jeremiah 10:2

Q: Why would it be useful to know what is going to happen to us in the future?

Q: What downsides could there be to this?

Q: What's Isaiah's advice? (Isaiah 8:19a) Why?

Q: Is there a better alternative? Try looking at Jeremiah 29:11.

## reflect

One day time will end and eternity begin. We live in the present and prepare for the future. Think about this verse:

*And even we Christians, although we have the Holy Spirit within us as a foretaste of future glory, also groan to be released from pain and suffering. We, too, wait anxiously for that day when God will give us our full rights as his children, including the new bodies he has promised us.*
**Romans 8:23**

Q: What kind of priorities does this mean we should have?

## re:action

**Give thanks together** that God loves us and can be trusted with our future. You might like to do this by **reading** part of Psalm 118 together. This psalm lends itself to being **said responsively**, either using one reader alternately with everyone else, or the group split into halves, one half for each part.

*Give thanks to the Lord, for he is good!*
**His faithful love endures forever.**
*Let the congregation of Israel repeat:*
**'His faithful love endures forever.'**
*Let Aaron's descendants, the priests, repeat:*
**'His faithful love endures forever.'**
*Let all who fear the Lord repeat:*
**'His faithful love endures forever.'**

*In my distress I prayed to the Lord,*
**and the Lord answered me and rescued me.**
*The Lord is for me, so I will not be afraid.*
**What can mere mortals do to me?**
*Yes, the Lord is for me; he will help me.*
**I will look in triumph at those who hate me.**
*It is better to trust the Lord*
**than to put confidence in people.**
*It is better to trust the Lord*
**than to put confidence in princes.**

**Psalm 118:1–9**

Next, **pray** for one another (silently or out loud, as preferred) that:

- God will speak to you through this series of discussions
- you will gain a greater understanding of how the future influences our lives today
- you will build deeper relationships with one another as you share this time together

# 2 Present hope, future certainty

*This confidence is like a strong and trustworthy anchor for our souls.*

**Hebrews 6:19**

## set the scene

Q: What invention would you most like to see appear sometime in the future? Why?

## explore

### 1 Future expectations

**Read**

Luke 12:16–21

Most of us have some expectation of what our life is going to involve in the future.

Q: As a young man, how do you think this farmer in the Bible passage would have imagined his immediate future? And his future further ahead?

Q: How would you describe his priorities at the time of the story?

*A person is a fool to store up earthly wealth but not have a rich relationship with God.*

**words of Jesus in Luke 12:21**

Q: How can we be certain that our priorities are God's priorities?


The man's hopes and expectations for his future altered his behaviour in the present. What hopes and expectations for the future do you think people hold when they say things like:

- 'Live now, pay later: that's my motto'?
- 'I hope everything will always be like this'?
- 'I rely on reading my horoscope every day'?

Our expectations for the future are not always met. Sometimes even realistic hopes may be dashed by unforeseen events. See if you can add at least one extra sentence to each of the following:

**Optimistic – but possible:**

- My football team will win promotion next season.
- I will be able to speak fluent French one day.

_____

_____

**Pretty much in vain:**

- Stalybridge Celtic will win the European Champions League.
- The 7.46 will arrive on time on a wet and wintry Monday morning.

_____

_____

**Realistic but unwelcome:**

- We will be older tomorrow.
- We will die one day.

_____

_____

**Hopeless:**

- We can't change anything, so why bother?

_____

_____

## 2 Deferred certainty

God offers us something different – not a future based on wishful thinking or hiding from reality, but a future built on his hope. We could call it 'deferred certainty' – a future that can't be unexpectedly derailed whatever may happen in our lives now.

**Read**

1 Corinthians 15:51–57
Ephesians 1:10
Titus 1:2

Q: What is the hope that God offers to us?

Q: How do we know God won't let us down?

Find three reasons in these next verses.

**Read**

Romans 15:4
1 Corinthians 15:12–20
Hebrews 10:23

Think back over your life.

Q: Can you remember specific times where you have experienced God's faithfulness to you? Talk about them with the group.

reflect

Q: What do you most fear about the future of the world as a whole?

Q: What do you most fear about your personal future?

Q: How can God's hope, the promise of ultimate victory over death and restored relationship with him, speak to us in these fears?

Q: What does his hope offer to those who face injustice or suffering in this world?

Q: How else could this hope affect the way we live today?

## re:action

Spend a few minutes **meditating** on this verse and then discuss with one another how these words make you feel:

*He will remove all of their sorrow, and there will be no more death or sorrow or crying or pain. For the old world and its evils are gone for ever.*

**Revelation 21:4**

**Make a list** together of some of the fears you listed earlier, either for the world or for yourselves. Being both realistic and optimistic, go on to **list** some practical things you can do to help with any of these situations. For example:

- is there someone you can write to?
- a group you could join?
- a way of offering practical help to someone?

**Pray together** for God's hope in the face of your fears for the world and for yourselves, and **ask** for his help in tackling some of those actions you've listed. If some or all of the group aren't confident praying aloud, everyone could say single words or sentences, naming the fear e.g. 'the threat of war' or 'being out of a job'. After each contribution, everyone else could respond by saying together: 'Lord, we want to know your hope in the face of this fear'.

# 3 The end of history

*Look! He comes with the clouds of heaven.*
*And everyone shall see him...*

**Revelation 1:7**

## set the scene

Many events in life require preparation, from going on holiday to taking exams. What three words would you use to describe the way you prepare for things?

1

2

3

Q: Why do you work this way?

## explore

### 1 The first coming

While we are preparing for the most dramatic moment in all history, the return of Jesus, his first coming was very different. Jesus was born almost unnoticed. An insignificant baby. In an insignificant place.

Divide into three groups to look at the next three Bible passages, and then share your findings.

**Read**

Luke 2:4–20
Luke 2:21–39
Matthew 2:1–12

Q: What do they tell us about:

- who Jesus was?
- why he came?
- who knew he was here?

Jesus came to earth to bring salvation, but as we look around us we see that his work is not yet finished and some prophecies about him are not yet fulfilled.

**Read**

Isaiah 11:1–10.

Here we see the promise of:
judgement (v4)
peace (v6)
everyone knowing the Lord (v9)
and all the nations turning to him (v10)

It is hard to claim that these things exist in our world as it is today, so we look forward to a time when that will change, at the Second Coming.

## 2 The Second Coming

Q: How do these next passages describe the Second Coming?

**Read**

Daniel 7:13,14
Matthew 24:27
Acts 1:9–11
1 Thessalonians 5:2
Revelation 1:7

Notice that all five passages have different authors/speakers and cover prophecy, historical record and teaching. The Bible is very clear about the reality of the Second Coming.

Q: In what ways will the Second Coming be different from the first?

Q: Why do you think the two comings of Jesus will be so different from each other?

The Second Coming is the decisive moment in history. It is the point connecting our time-bound world with the life of the world to come. In 1 Corinthians 15:24 Paul says, 'after that the end will come...' But what is it all for?

Q: Identify four reasons for the Second Coming in these groups of verses. You might like to tackle this in four groups and share your findings.

**Read**

Revelation 20:10 and 1 Corinthians 15:25
Matthew 25:31–33 and 2 Timothy 4:1
John 5:28,29a and 1 Corinthians 15:52
2 Peter 3:13 and Romans 8:21

## reflect

Some people claim that Jesus won't make a physical, visible return but comes back 'spiritually' through the lives of those who believe in him.

Q: How do you respond to such views? Does it really matter whether Jesus comes back physically or not?

**Read**

Matthew 24:45–51

Q: How should we be living as we wait for Jesus' return?

In a few minutes of quiet, here are two questions for you to answer on your own:

Q: Are you living in this way?

Q: If not, what needs to change?

# re:action

This session began by looking at the coming of Jesus, celebrated at Christmas. Christmas is a time of year that many enjoy – and some dread. **Discuss** how you all feel about Christmas; and what differences you think knowing Jesus makes about those feelings. **Think about** any individuals or groups you know who find Christmas a difficult time of year (because of loneliness, for example), and **decide** on one thing you could do as an individual or group to make next Christmas better for someone.

Whatever the time of year, you could take a few minutes now to **celebrate** that first coming together. You could:

- **sing** someone's favourite carol

- **read** part of the Christmas story together, perhaps using *The Message* (American paraphrase of the Bible) or a translation that the group isn't familiar with

- **pray** together, **thanking** God in your own words for Jesus coming to us

# 4  Approaching the end

*For you know quite well
that the day of the Lord will come unexpectedly,
like a thief in the night.*

**1 Thessalonians 5:2**

## set the scene

Q: How do you handle waiting for things?

For each question, select the answer which is most like you.

1 You've been waiting in the supermarket for ages when there's a hold-up with the person in front of you. All the other queues are miles long. Do you:

   a  abandon your shopping even though you really need it?

   b  tap your foot, tut and sigh loudly?

   c  smile at the shop assistant and the person in front of you to show them you know it's not their fault?

   d  rant and moan to everyone in earshot?

   e  treat it as an opportunity to practise your rusty gift of patience and pray for help?

2 The bus is late. Very late. Very, very late. Do you:

   a  give up and walk the three miles to work?

   b  call a taxi on your mobile phone?

   c  give up, go home and call in sick?

   d  wait and wait and wait and arrive late, hassled and bad-tempered?

   e  stay cool... what wait? You were making the most of the time by memorising some Bible verses!

3 Think back to being a small child with Christmas coming. Did you:

   a  ransack the house looking for hidden presents?

   b  never think about presents... after all, it's a holy day?

c drive everyone mad by asking how long to Christmas three times a day from October 1st?

d get so excited about such a fabulous day that it could never match up to your expectations?

e have a life so busy with other things you never realised Christmas was coming until the last minute?

Q: Do you think people would describe you as good at waiting for things?

Q: What is the worst wait you've ever had to make?

## 1 Impatient people

We are waiting for Jesus, living in the time between his two comings, a time often described as 'the Last Days' (2 Peter 3:3). Even in the time of the New Testament some people were struggling to wait patiently and seeking explanations for the delay.

### Response to delay: deciding he's already returned

Some people in the days of the early church thought Jesus could have returned already and been missed (2 Thessalonians 2:1,2). Even today people claim that they are, or follow, the true Messiah: Jesus already returned to earth. Look at these three ways we can be sure that these people are following the wrong man.

**Read**

Matthew 24:4,5,23–25
Matthew 24:26,27 and Revelation 1:7
1 John 4:1–3

## Response to delay: scoffing and doubting

### Read

2 Peter 3:3–9

Q: How does Peter answer the people who found the wait hard and so resorted to scoffing?

Q: If God is not slow but patient, does this mean we have to wait until everyone has come to know him before Jesus will return?

## 2 Signs of the times

### Read

Matthew 24:1–14

Q: What events does Jesus describe as a part of life in the last days; things we should be expecting to happen?

Q: How does he say we should respond to these things?
Look particularly at verses 4, 6, and 13.

**Reality check**  Since Jesus spoke these words, every generation has believed that the world has reached its lowest point and the end is near. However, Jesus makes it clear that these things are **not** special signs of the imminent end of the world, but a constant part of life in the Last Days – that is all the time between Jesus' first coming and his return to earth. In his book *End of Story?* Stephen Travis describes this passage from Matthew not as giving precise signs we should look for, but as a kind of hazard warning.

### Read

Matthew 24:36–44

Q: What does this passage make clear about the timing of Jesus' return?

Here we see that life at the time of Jesus' return will be carrying on **as usual**. Our world faces possible terminal dangers from environmental change, meteorites, biological and chemical terrorism and nuclear war. As we pointed out in the **Intro**, when the millennium approached, people ranging from the truly wild and wacky edges of life through to those from some established churches suggested that the year 2000 would mark either the return of Jesus or at least an alien invasion. Films such as *Armageddon, Deep Impact* and *Independence Day* built interest in possible doomsday scenarios.

Q: Has there ever been a time when you feared that the world was about to be destroyed?

Q: How can we use the interest in 'end of the world' films and books etc to share with people what the Bible says about Jesus' return?

Q: What dangers might lie in interpreting world events as warning signs for God's imminent return?

## reflect

**Read**

2 Peter 3:10–14

Q: Are you looking forward to Jesus' return? Why/why not?

Q: Peter encourages us to *hurry it along*. How can we do this?

These next verses shed some light on different things we could do.

**Read**

Matthew 6:9,10
Matthew 24:14
Acts 3:19–20 and 2 Peter 3:9
2 Peter 3:11

re:action

A question for quiet reflection on your own:

Q: Which of these do you most need to work on?

It is possible to spend **too little time** being prepared for the return of Jesus. It is possible to spend **too much time** thinking about it. Jesus has warned us that whatever disasters and problems we see around us and experience ourselves, we are not to believe that God has lost the plot. He remains in control, working out his purposes for the world.

## re:action

We live in a very unsettled world. Take a couple of the week's national and local newspapers and share the pages out. In pairs **choose** two or three headlines from current news – both in the wider world and closer to home. Join up as a whole group again and **decide** on three or four issues that you would particularly like to **pray** for. Try to cover a variety of stories, or at least different angles on the same story.

If you prefer, you could **watch** a videoed news bulletin, stopping the video between each story to **pray**.

End by **reading** this passage together, remembering that however gloomy and frightening the news is, God is still in ultimate control.

*Say this to those who worship other gods: 'Your so-called gods, who did not make the heavens and earth, will vanish from the earth.'*

*But God made the earth by his power,*
*   and he preserves it by his wisdom.*
*He has stretched out the heavens*
*   by his understanding.*
*When he speaks, there is thunder in the heavens.*
*   He causes the clouds to rise over the earth.*
*He sends the lightning with the rain*
*   and releases the wind from his storehouses.*
*Compared to him, all people are foolish*
*   and have no knowledge at all!*
*They make idols, but the idols will disgrace their makers,*
*   for they are frauds.*
*   They have no life or power in them.*

*Idols are worthless; they are lies!*
*The time is coming when they will all be destroyed.*
*But the God of Israel is no idol!*
*He is the Creator of everything that exists,*
*including Israel, his own special possession.*
*The Lord Almighty is his name!*

**Jeremiah 10:11–16**

# 5 The moment of truth

*God is ready to help you right now. Today is the day of salvation.*

**2 Corinthians 6:2b**

set the scene

**Imagine it** Pat Bloggs has recently started coming to your church and doesn't really know anyone yet. Last Sunday the Vicar leaned on you to go and speak to Pat, so you went and chatted for a few minutes over coffee.

Q: What kinds of things help you to build up an initial picture of what Pat is like?

Q: Do you think first impressions of people are reliable or not? If you can, give some examples from your own life.

## explore

### 1 God's judgement

Whatever use we make of first impressions, God does not rely on them nor does he judge us by the parts of us we put on public view.

**Read**

1 Samuel 16:1–13

Q: What was Samuel's reaction to the arrival of Eliab (v6)?

Q: How did God make his choice?

Things haven't changed since David's time. God still judges us on the same basis. 1 Corinthians 4:5 says,

*So be careful not to jump to conclusions before the Lord returns as to whether or not someone is faithful. When the Lord comes, he will bring our deepest secrets to light and will reveal our private motives. And then God will give to everyone whatever praise is due.*

## 2 The final judgement

After Jesus returns, there will be a final judgement. The certainty of that is confirmed in the Bible.

**Read**

Hebrews 9:27
2 Peter 3:7–9
2 Corinthians 5:10

Q: What do you imagine Judgement Day will be like?

We all come to judgement as sinners.

*When Adam sinned, sin entered the entire human race. Adam's sin brought death, so death spread to everyone, for everyone sinned.*

**Romans 5:12**

Q: So, how does God judge?

**Read**

Ephesians 2:8,9
Matthew 25:31–46

Q: How does Jesus divide the sheep from the goats?

A key verse in this passage is v40: *Whatever you did for one of the least of these brothers of mine…* A common interpretation of this passage assumes that good works done for those in need reveal a person's faith and decide a person's future destiny. Another view is that it is the way people treat Jesus' followers that really matters.

Q: Why does the way people treat Jesus' followers matter so much? Go back to Matthew 10:40.

In this passage the sheep and goats are judged on their actions.

Q: Is it possible to combine the teaching of this passage with the emphasis elsewhere that salvation is through faith alone? You may find James 2:14–18 and Ephesians 2:8,9 helpful in answering this.

## 3 Two problems

### Problem 1: A God of love?

Q: Is it possible to reconcile these three statements?

- God does not want anyone to perish (2 Peter 3:9b)
- God loves us all (John 3:16,17 and Romans 5:7,8)
- Jesus says that some people will end up in the eternal fire (Matthew 25:41)

One way is to suggest that in the end God will allow everyone into heaven. Does the evidence support this idea? In the verse from Matthew, who is *the eternal fire* meant for?

It was not God's original intention that any person should end up facing destruction, but the New Testament does not teach 'universalism', that is, everyone ending up in heaven.

### Read

2 Peter 2:12,13
Romans 1:28–32

And here it is, put vividly, in *The Message:*

*This is the crisis we're in; God-light streamed into the world, but men and women everywhere ran for the darkness.*

*They went for the darkness because they were not really interested in pleasing God. Everyone who makes a practice of doing evil, addicted to denial and illusion, hates God-light and won't come near it, fearing a painful exposure. But anyone working and living in truth and reality*

*welcomes God-light so the work can be seen for the God-work it is.*
John 3:18–21

Q: Who is rejecting who in this passage?

While they are alive people can change their mind about Jesus at any time, but the Bible describes no such opportunity beyond death.

*If a person is ashamed of me and my message in these adulterous and sinful days, I, the Son of Man, will be ashamed of that person when I return in the glory of my Father with the holy angels.*
Mark 8:38

Some people find it unfair that a person could accept Jesus on their death-bed, after a lifetime of rejecting him.

Q: Do you agree with the view that it is unfair? Why does God allow this? Check your views against Romans 5:15.

So, while there will be a final judgement, it is clear that our destiny on that day is decided here on earth, through our response to Jesus now. It is not so much that Jesus rejects people, but that people reject Jesus.

**Problem 2: What about those who haven't ever heard about Jesus?**

**Read**
Romans 2:12–16
Luke 12:47,48

Q: Do these passages suggest that everyone will be treated the same way at judgement?

Think about this: 'If a Hindu finds salvation, it is not by virtue of being a good Hindu, any more than a Christian is saved by being a good Christian.'

Q: Is it possible for people from other religious to be saved?

re:action

**Read**

Acts 4:12

We can be sure that God's justice will be seen by everyone to be fair.

*Will not the Judge of all the earth do right?*
**Genesis 18:25 (NIV)**

Q: What would you say to someone who thought it better not to share the gospel with others in case they rejected it to protect them from then facing God's wrath on the Day of Judgement?

reflect

What really matters? Sin is a serious thing. It cuts us off from a holy God. What happens to us at the judgement is dependent on our response to Jesus here on earth in our daily lives.

Jesus warns us against complacency.

*On judgment day many will tell me, 'Lord, Lord, we prophesied in your name and cast out demons in your name and performed many miracles in your name.' But I will reply, 'I never knew you. Go away; the things you did were unauthorised'.*
**Matthew 7:22,23**

However, this should not lead us to doubt our salvation, but remind us that 'being religious' and doing 'religious things' will not be enough. Regardless of how we feel, only trust in Jesus will bring the certainty of salvation to us and to those we care for.

What really matters is how we are with God – we can't be certain about anyone else.

## re:action

Spend a few minutes of **quiet thinking** about your all-important right relationship with God. **Make a mental list** of areas you can think of that might be damaging that relationship and need sorting out. **Ask** the other members of your group to **pray** for you as you try to deal with them. **Share** as much or as little as seems appropriate and you are comfortable with.

But it's not just our relationship with God we need to be careful about. Sin damages all our relationships. **Sit in silence** together for a short time, allowing God to bring things you've done wrong into your mind, which may have caused harm or a broken relationship with someone else. Then, **pray** a prayer of repentance for these things together, either using your own words or choosing one from a service book you use, or from another book of prayers.

As a reminder that Jesus' death on the cross is the source of our forgiveness, cut out small paper or card crosses for everyone and write on them:

*...he purchased our freedom through the blood of his Son, and our sins are forgiven.*

**Ephesians 1:7**

# 6 Out of the shadows

*... we are looking forward to the new heavens, and new earth he has promised, a world where everyone is right with God.*

**2 Peter 3:13**

## set the scene

Q: If you had never set foot in a church, what impressions of heaven might you have gathered? Refer back to the quotation from Laurie Lee in the **Intro** right at the beginning of this booklet.

The Bible doesn't really speak of 'going to heaven' when we die, **but** of being part of God's new kingdom.

## explore

### 1 What will I be like in heaven?

Q: How do you recognise the person sitting next to you as definitely them?

Q: If you met someone after 40 years and their physical appearance had changed completely, how would you know it was them?

**Still me physically** In heaven we will still be recognisably, but differently, us.

**Read**

1 Corinthians 15:37–44, 50–53

Q: Why will we need a new body?

Jesus was obviously different after the resurrection: he could appear and disappear at will, he didn't want people to hold onto him and at times people were slow to recognise him, but he was still himself.

**Read**

John 20:14–17, 26–28.

Heaven is a physical world. We will not be 'less' than we are now; it is not just about the immortality of the soul but of the body too.

**Still me in terms of my personality**  Jesus remained the same person that he had been before death. Discuss this statement: the more we grow like Jesus now, the less there will be to renew beyond death and the more recognisably us we shall remain.

Q: Do you agree or disagree?


**Still me in terms of my memories**  Memory forms us as people; in diseases such as Alzheimer's where memory is lost, friends and family often feel that the real person is gone. Jesus retained his memories of life on earth; so it seems probable that we will still have some memory of life now when we are part of the renewed people of the new heaven and the new earth.

## 2 What will heaven be like?

Fortunately it won't just be sitting around singing and playing harps for millions of years! The Bible gives us several images of heaven, giving us clues as to what life will be like there. List your findings from the verses below.

**Read**

Hebrews 11:10
Matthew 8:11,12
John 14:23
Matthew 25:34,35
John 14:2

In heaven **we will be in God's presence** – fulfilling the very purpose for which we were created, to know and be with God.

**Read**

Romans 8:19–21

In heaven **there will be an end to all that is evil.**

**Read**

Revelation 21:3,4
Isaiah 25:7,8
Revelation 20:10

In heaven **we will be a community** – fulfilling God's design of us as people meant for relationships with others.

Q: What things bring you most joy and pleasure in this life?


Q: How many of them involve the contributions of other people in some way?


How much more will this be true when our social relationships are perfect!

In heaven **we will have a purpose** – fulfilling God's plans for me through service to him and others.

**Read**

Revelation 22:3

In some way we will be contributing to the new world as we are called to do in this world.

## 3 Is there a downside?

The Bible makes it very clear that not everyone is going to be part of the new heaven and the new earth.

**Read**

Revelation 22:14,15
Matthew 25:41,46
2 Thessalonians 1:6–10

Q: What do these verses tell us about the experience of those who reject Jesus?

There are few descriptions in the Bible of exactly what hell will involve, except in the picture-language of Revelation. Some of those that do exist seem contradictory, especially if we are trying to interpret images literally. While Matthew's Gospel describes a place of eternal fire, Peter talks of total darkness, for example.

**Read**

Matthew 25:41
2 Peter 2:17

Some people believe that hell will last forever. Others believe that it won't. The key points in that debate are:

- Immortality is a gift from God, not an automatic part of human experience – so, it is argued, those who love God are granted eternal life and those who don't go out of existence.
- 'Eternal' punishment may describe the results of judgement, rather than a continuing experience of judgement. So this would mean that, once decided, a person's fate cannot be changed.
- Eternal punishment requires that heaven and hell exist along-side each other forever.
- Some believe that the idea of eternal punishment cannot be reconciled with the view that one day all evil *will be defeated and God will be utterly supreme over everything everywhere* (1 Corinthians 15:28).

## reflect

**Read**

Luke 13:22–30

Here we see a reminder that in the end this discussion on heaven and hell is not about other people. It is not about the just fate of individuals such as Stalin and Hitler. It is about our personal future – your future and mine. Jesus challenges us to follow him through the narrow door and to do so before it is too late.

*…the throne of God and of the Lamb will be there, and his servants will worship him. And they will see his face, and his name will be written on their foreheads. And there will be no night there – no needs for lamps or*

*sun – for the Lord God will shine on them. And they will reign for ever and ever.*

**Revelation 22:3–5**

## re:action

**Think about** those you see regularly who are not yet Christians – perhaps in your home, at work, at the local shop, at the bus stop... **choose** two or three you would particularly like to pray for and have an opportunity to share Jesus with. **Write** down their names, perhaps on a card that you could keep in your Bible or somewhere you'll see it often. **Think** of one possible next step you could take with each of these people.

Be realistic about those next steps – you're unlikely to be able to share your faith with someone if you don't know them well already. You might need:

- time to get to know them better before you can talk to them about Jesus
- an opening to tell them you are a Christian
- an opportunity to invite them to an event at your church

Whatever it is, **write** that down on the card next to their name.

**Pray together** for these people and your next steps with them. **Continue to pray** for these people over the next few weeks. **Report** on anything that happens with the rest of the group.

The group might like to think about running their own event for interested friends that aren't yet Christians. Or plan an event that the whole church could take part in and support.

For example:

- you could **show a video** or **go to a film** and then discuss it. It doesn't have to be a 'Christian' film, just one that could be used to lead naturally into a discussion of spiritual things
- you could **hold a barbecue**, with one person explaining why they became a Christian
- you could **go to a church or other Christian event** together

**Discuss** what your group could do, even if you want to plan it for some time in the future. Knowing that such an event is coming up will help to focus your prayers for the people named on the cards.

Some advice:

- **Be realistic** about the kind of event that you could run.
- Stick to something the whole group would enjoy doing.
- Don't be too ambitious; if it is your first try at something like this – **start small**.
- **Make sure** that those you invite understand what they are coming to; don't hide the Christian element.

# 7 One foot beyond the grave

*In keeping with his promise, we are looking forward to a new heaven
and a new earth, the home of righteousness.
So then, dear friends, as you are looking forward to this,
make every effort to be found spotless, blameless
and at peace with him.*

**2 Peter 3:13,14**

## set the scene

Q: What are you like at following instructions – for example for
building bookcases or finding your way to a new place? Do you
stick to them closely or do you plunge in and hope it works out
OK?

Q: Have you ever ended up with a total disaster, despite trying to
follow the instructions? Describe it to the group.

## explore

The life of the new heaven and new earth give us a blueprint for how
our world should have turned out. One day that original plan will be
restored. Knowing that can make significant difference to us today.

## 1 Differences in our relationships

**Our relationship with God** God's kingdom is not just confined to
some future date beyond the end of time. It begins here, despite the
limitations of our present existence. We are called to be God's
demonstration models, showing others what it means to be a resident
of his kingdom.

Q: How do we do this?

**Read**

1 Peter 4:7–11

Q: Why does Peter encourage us to be clear-minded and self-controlled when we pray? Can we still pray effectively when we are anything but these things?

**Our love for each other** Love between Christians is not just about having a natural liking or affection for people.

Q: Why do you think Peter encourages love for each other above all?

Q: How can we express love to those who we might naturally prefer to ignore or avoid?

Q: How do you feel about opening your home to others?

Q: In what ways does hospitality encourage openness and acceptance between people in the church?

Q: Are there other benefits?

**Our service to the Body of Christ** This is another way of showing love to God's people: sharing the gift(s) God has given us in response to the needs around us.

Q: How can we encourage people to discover and use the gifts God has given them?

Q: What are the dangers of speaking or doing things in our own strength, not God's?

The next three questions will need a few minutes of quiet reflection. Share your thoughts with the group if you feel you'd like their support and prayer.

Q: Where do you think you are most effectively living God's way?


Q: Where do you most need to change or grow further?


Q: What one practical thing could you do to develop in that area?


## 2 Differences in our relationship with the world

Peter describes us as foreigners and aliens (1 Peter 2:11), not citizens of this world but of the coming kingdom. In the past some have interpreted this to mean that they could ignore social or political injustice, focusing only on making new Christians. Others have tackled people's social needs but neglected their spiritual needs.

Those who oppress others will be judged at the end of time, those who suffer now will see justice done then.

Q: Why might it still be important to try and overcome oppression and suffering in our world?


reflect

**Reality check** The values and life of the new heaven and the new earth to come show us what God wanted for our world too. By taking even tiny steps in that direction, we are furthering his purposes for our world and for all people, even if ultimately the full effects will only come as God's gift to all his creation.

Q: Where should Christians put their main energies?
- actively attacking oppression and injustice?
- building up the church?
- spreading the gospel?

Q: If our present world is 'passing away', how much does our over-use of the world's resources matter?

Q: How could we play a greater part in the overthrow of injustice and in the conservation of the world's resources?
- as individuals?
- as a group?
- as a church?

## re:action

## Pray together
- about anything discussed
- for those caught up in the suffering and sin of our present world
- for those who are trying to help them
- for the ideas you've had for ways to help
- for the spread of God's end-time values in and through your life

Q: What have you found to be the best thing about doing this series of studies together?

Q: Is there anything you have learned/discovered that has made a difference to you?

God's people are streaks of dawn in the darkened sky, lights that show the hope of God's future return and a full establishing of his kingdom. Through the power of his Spirit, we show others what it means to be a resident of that kingdom and slowly move the world towards its final destiny.

re:action

Read or sing these verses together:

*At the name of Jesus*
*Every knee shall bow;*
*Every tongue confess him*
*King of glory now;*
*'Tis the Father's pleasure*
*We should call Him Lord*
*Who from the beginning*
*Was the mighty Word.*

*Brothers, this Lord Jesus*
*Shall return again.*
*With the Father's glory,*
*With his angel-train.*
*For all wreaths of empire*
*Meet upon his brow.*
*And our hearts confess Him*
*King of glory now.*

**Re:action small group Bible resources by Kate Hayes**

## Others in the series

### For the tough times

*Does God care when I'm hurting?*
Whether it's thousands killed in a terrorist attack as you watch on TV, your next door neighbour on chemo for cancer, or your best friend's marriage on shaky ground... there's no escaping the issue of suffering. Maybe you want to shout at God that's it's just so unfair! Just what's it all for?

**ISBN 1 85999 622 1**

### Chosen for change

*Am I part of God's big plan?*
Like it or not, you're living in the 'me' culture. Are you comfortable with going it alone, taking care of 'Number One', cashing in on 'your rights' and turning a blind eye to responsibilities? What about sharing... caring... belonging... teamwork... community? Are you ready to serve not self – but society?

**ISBN 1 85999 623 X**

### The possibility of purpose

*What's the meaning of my life?*
A treadmill existence of deadlines and pressures? Or a kaleidoscope of amazing opportunities? What's your take on daily life? Do you see yourself as a meaningless cosmic dust speck? Or a significant mover in a masterplan? Your view affects your motivation, your self-esteem, your priorities, your everyday choices...

**ISBN 1 85999 620 5**

**Available from all good Christian bookshops** *or*
- phone SU's mail order line: 01908 856006
- email info@scriptureunion.org.uk
- fax 01908 856020
- log on to www.scriptureunion.org.uk
- or write to SU Mail Order:
  PO Box 5148, Milton Keynes MLO, MK2 2YX

## ALSO FROM SCRIPTURE UNION

## BODYBUILDERS
small group Bible resources

Six booklets, six sessions in each - designed for even the busiest small group leader! A complete 'off the shelf' resource. Simply choose from the flexible menu-style approach which includes notes for leaders, icebreakers, ideas for worship and prayer, interactive and in-depth Bible study material, photocopiable response sheets plus 'take home' material.

Taking interactivity to a new level, BODYBUILDERS provide really fresh and creative ways for your group to access the Bible together. Informal but challenging, the series encourages group members to grow in their faith and build strong relationships, by drawing on their own stories and relating personal experience to the principles of biblical living.

## Relationship Building
### - growing a caring and committed community
**Lance Pierson**
It's impossible to live daily life without constant interaction with the people around us: family, neighbours, friends or workmates. To help you and your group develop the skills needed to build healthy relationships.
**ISBN 1 85999 582 9**

## True Security
### - welcoming life's changes as opportunities
**Lance Pierson**
Do we fear change because we have mis-placed our emotional security? This material challenges you and your group to find security in God himself, to welcome any kind of change as an opportunity to deepen that trust, and to discover strength and support in the community of the church.
**ISBN 1 85999 583 7**

## Surviving under pressure
### - finding strength in the tough times
**Christopher Griffiths & Stephen Hathway**

We live in high-pressure days, bombarded with conflicting views and influences that can be obstacles to adopting lifestyles that truly reflect Christian values and principles. Aimed at equipping Christian believers to stand firm even on the roughest ground.

**ISBN 1 85999 587 X**

## Designed for great things
### - wrestling with human nature
**Anton Baumohl**

Human beings - beautiful and unique yet rebellious and capable of evil! Only the Christian view of man makes real sense of the good and bad things about being human. Interactive material to help you and your group to discover your true potential in Christ.

**ISBN 1 85999 585 3**

## A Fresh Encounter
### - meeting the real Jesus
**David Bolster**

Some were intrigued, attracted to him, accepted, loved and followed him; others were afraid of him, were disturbed by him or rejected him. To challenge you and your group to extend your understanding of who Jesus is and what that means in everyday life.

**ISBN 1 85999 586 1**

## Living for the King
### - growing God's rule in our world
**'Tricia Williams**

'God in control? It doesn't look like it!' Is that your reaction to the suffering and injustice you see in the world. A look at key issues which have immediate relevance for those who want to be involved in the risky and exciting business of being God's community here and now.

**ISBN 1 85999 584 5**

## For a free catalogue of Bible resources from Scripture Union:

- phone SU's mail order line: 01908 856006
- email info@scriptureunion.org.uk
- fax 01908 856020
- log on to www.scriptureunion.org.uk
- or write to SU Mail Order:
  PO Box 5148, Milton Keynes MLO, MK2 2YX

You might also like to request free samplers from our range of personal Bible reading guides:

**ENCOUNTER WITH GOD** - provides a thought-provoking, in-depth approach to Bible reading, relating Biblical truth to contemporary issues. The writers are experienced Bible teachers, often well known.

**DAILY BREAD** - aims to help you enjoy, explore and apply the Bible. Practical comments relate the Bible to everyday life.

**CLOSER TO GOD** - experiential, relational, radical and dynamic, this publication takes a creative and reflective approach to Bible reading with an emphasis on renewal.

SU also produces Bible reading notes for children, teens and young adults. Do ask for details.